Middle School
Internet Research Projects (Grades 5-8)

The Alaska State Quarter

Search online for several interes...
words and numbers on the U...

ONLINE SOURCES...

What do we know about time travel?

Use a computer, tablet or phone to sear...

ONLINE SOURCES...

Who is Sally Ride?

Use a laptop, tablet or phone to access the internet
and explore this famous Californian.

Age:

Gender:

Place of birth:

Ethnicity:

Search for interesting facts about this famous Californian: major accomplishments in life, odd jobs, family and marriage, childhood experiences, accidents, anything that you find odd or strange:

ONLINE SOURCES OF INFORMATION:

101 printable activities

C. Mahoney

Life is about choices...

What do we know about time travel?

Use a <u>computer</u>, <u>tablet</u> or <u>phone</u> to search online for answers to this question.

ONLINE SOURCES OF INFORMATION:

The Alaska State Quarter

Search online for several interesting facts about <u>animals</u>, <u>plants</u>, <u>words</u> and <u>numbers</u> on the U.S. quarter honoring Alaska.

_____

_____

_____

_____

_____

_____

_____

_____

_____

_____

ONLINE SOURCES OF INFORMATION:

⬇

1)	2)	3)

Countries in The Caribbean Islands

Use a phone, tablet or laptop to identify some of the largest and most populous countries in the Caribbean:

Aruba, the Bahamas, Barbados, Cuba, Curacao, Cayman Islands, Dominican Republic, Grenada, Haiti, Jamaica, Martinique, Puerto Rico, Saint Lucia, Trinidad and Tobago, U.S. Virgin Islands

Who is Sally Ride?

Use a laptop, tablet or phone to access the internet and explore this famous Californian.

Age:

Gender:

Place of birth:

Ethnicity:

Search for interesting facts about this famous Californian: major accomplishments in life, odd jobs, family and marriage, childhood experiences, accidents, anything that you find odd or strange:

ONLINE SOURCES OF INFORMATION:

The Flag of Egypt

Draw the **national flag** of Egypt. Use colored pencils, crayons, or markers. Be neat and accurate.

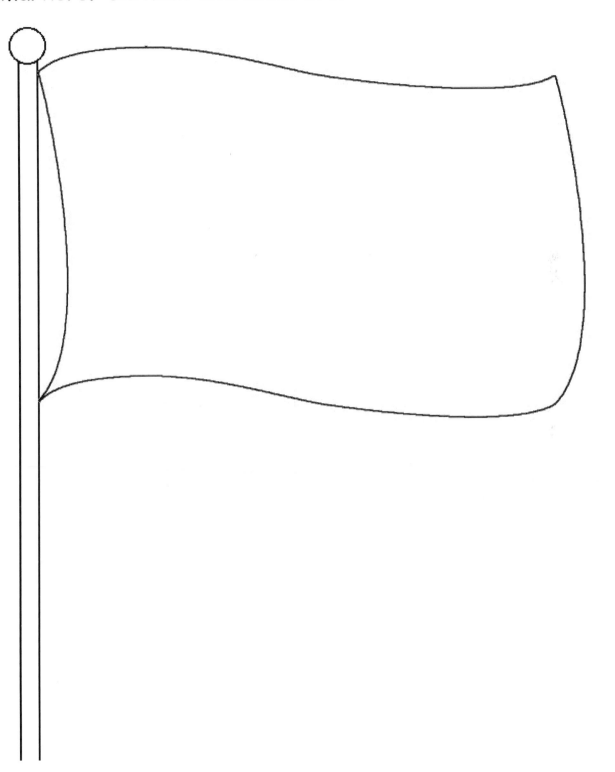

Who is Elie Wiesel?

Use a phone, tablet or laptop to list five important facts.

1._____

_____

_____

SOURCE: _____

2._____

_____

_____

SOURCE: _____

3._____

_____

_____

SOURCE: _____

4._____

_____

_____

SOURCE: _____

5._____

_____

_____

SOURCE: _____

The Indigenous Peoples of America

1.

2.

3.

4.

5.

6.

7.

8.

9.

10.

ONLINE SOURCES OF INFORMATION:

1)	2)	3)

Countries in North America

Use a phone, tablet or laptop to identify some of the largest and most populous countries in North America:

Belize, Canada, Costa Rica, Cuba, Dominican Republic, El Salvador, Greenland, Guatemala, Haiti, Honduras, Jamaica, Mexico, Nicaragua, Panama, United States of America,

Who is Sojourner Truth?

Use a phone, tablet or laptop to discover why we honor this person.

_____

_____

_____

_____

_____

_____

_____

_____

_____

_____

_____

_____

_____

_____

_____

ONLINE SOURCES OF INFORMATION:

⬇

1)

2)

3)

Who is Stephen Hawking?

Use a <u>computer</u>, <u>tablet</u> or <u>phone</u> to search online for information about this well-known scientist.

Details about his life

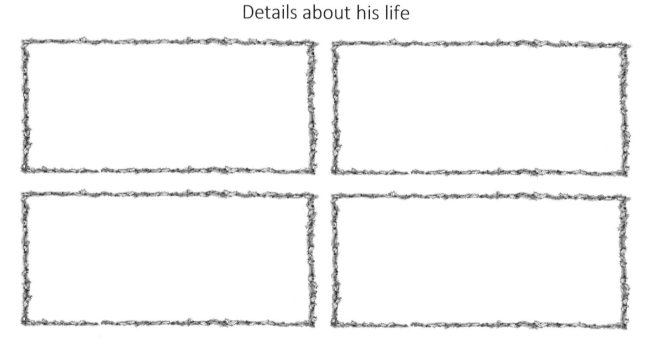

Accomplishments he is most noted for:

Who is Julia Child?

Use a laptop, tablet or phone to access the internet and explore this famous cook.

Age:

Gender:

Place of birth:

Ethnicity:

Search for interesting facts about this famous cook: major accomplishments in life, odd jobs, family and marriage, childhood experiences, accidents, anything that you find odd or strange:

1.

2.

3.

4.

ONLINE SOURCES OF INFORMATION:

The Sea Star

Use a phone, tablet or laptop to answer these questions.

What it eats…

Fact #1: _____

_____

Fact #2: _____

_____

SOURCE: _____

Where it lives…

Fact #1: _____

_____

Fact #2: _____

_____

SOURCE: _____

Family life…

Fact #1: _____

_____

Fact #2: _____

_____

SOURCE: _____

Connection to humans…

Fact #1: _____

_____

Fact #2: _____

_____

SOURCE: _____

The Octopus

Use a phone, tablet or laptop to answer these questions.

Is the octopus dangerous to humans?

☐ – YES

☐ – NO

How does an octopus eat?

Is an octopus smart?

YES NO

How long does an octopus live?

24 365 7

ONLINE SOURCES OF INFORMATION:

⬇

1)	2)	3)

Who is Joe DiMaggio?

Use a laptop, tablet or phone to access the internet and explore this famous athlete.

Age:

Gender:

Place of birth:

Ethnicity:

Search for interesting facts about this famous athlete: major accomplishments in life, odd jobs, family and marriage, childhood experiences, accidents, anything that you find odd or strange:

1

2

3

4

5

ONLINE SOURCES OF INFORMATION:

North Carolina

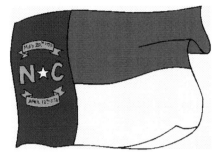

Use a phone, tablet or laptop to answer these questions.

1. What is the state motto? _____

2. How many people live there? _____

3. How big is this state? _____

4. Who is the governor? _____

5. Where is the capitol? _____

6. Which city is the largest? _____

7. How long have they been a state? _____

8. What job or work is most common? _____

9. What religion is most popular? _____

10. What are three interesting things you learned? _____

_____

_____

_____

_____

_____

_____

_____

_____

SOURCE: _____

SOURCE: _____

SOURCE: _____

The Rattlesnake

Use a phone, tablet or laptop to answer these questions.

Is the rattlesnake dangerous to humans?

☐ - YES

☐ - NO

_____
_____
_____

How does a rattlesnake eat?

_____
_____
_____
_____

Is a rattlesnake smart?

YES
OR
NO

_____
_____
_____

How long does a rattlesnake live?

_____
_____
_____
_____

ONLINE SOURCES OF INFORMATION:

1)

2)

3)

The Map of North Carolina

Use a phone, tablet or laptop to identify important places in this state: mountains, rivers, lakes, cities, historical sites, neighboring states, or bordering bodies of water.

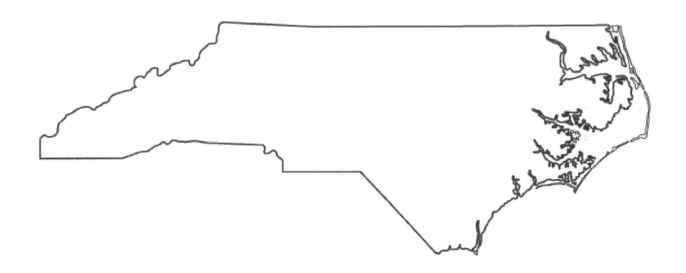

Who is Jack London?

Use a laptop, tablet or phone to access the internet and explore this famous writer.

Age:

Gender:

Place of birth:

Ethnicity:

Search for interesting facts about this famous writer: major accomplishments in life, odd jobs, family and marriage, childhood experiences, accidents, anything that you find odd or strange:

ONLINE SOURCES OF INFORMATION:

The Pyramids of Ancient Egypt

Search online for information about the pyramids of ancient Egypt: how they got built, when, by whom, their purpose, what they're made of, etc.

_____

_____

_____

_____

_____

_____

_____

_____

_____

_____

_____

_____

_____

_____

_____

_____

_____

_____

_____

_____

_____

_____

_____

_____

Texas

Use a phone, tablet or laptop to answer these questions.

1. What is the state motto? _____

2. How many people live there? _____

3. How big is this state? _____

4. Who is the governor? _____

5. Where is the capitol? _____

6. Which city is the largest? _____

7. How long have they been a state? _____

8. What job or work is most common? _____

9. What religion is most popular? _____

10. What are three interesting things you learned? _____

_____

_____

_____

_____

_____

_____

_____

_____

SOURCE: _____

SOURCE: _____

SOURCE: _____

What is the job of the President?

List ten activities or actions that a President is responsible for:

1.

2.

3.

4.

5.

6.

7.

8.

9.

10.

SOURCES:

_____

_____

Countries in Asia

Use a phone, tablet or laptop to identify some of the largest and most populous countries in Asia:

Afghanistan, Bangladesh, China, Cambodia, Hong Kong, India, Indonesia, Iran, Iraq, Isreal, Japan, Jordan, Kazakhstan, Laos, Lebanon, Malyasia, Mongolia, Myanmar, Nepal, North Korea, Oman, Pakistan, Philippines, Qatar, Russia, Saudi Arabia, Singapore, South Korea, Syria, Taiwan, Thailand, Turkey, United Arab Empirates, Uzbekistan, Vietnam, Yemen

School

Use a phone, tablet or laptop to answer these questions.

1. How big is the biggest PENCIL? _____

_____

SOURCE: _____

2. How big is the biggest BOOK? _____

_____

SOURCE: _____

3. How big is the biggest SCHOOL? _____

_____

SOURCE: _____

4. How big is the biggest BUS? _____

_____

SOURCE: _____

5. How big is the biggest RULER? _____

_____

SOURCE: _____

6. How big is the biggest ERASER? _____

_____

SOURCE: _____

Fish

Use a phone, tablet or laptop to answer these questions.

What is the smallest fish?

_____
_____
_____

What is the biggest fish?

_____
_____
_____

What is the fastest fish?

_____
_____
_____

Which fish lives the longest?

_____
_____
_____

source: _____
source: _____
source: _____
source: _____

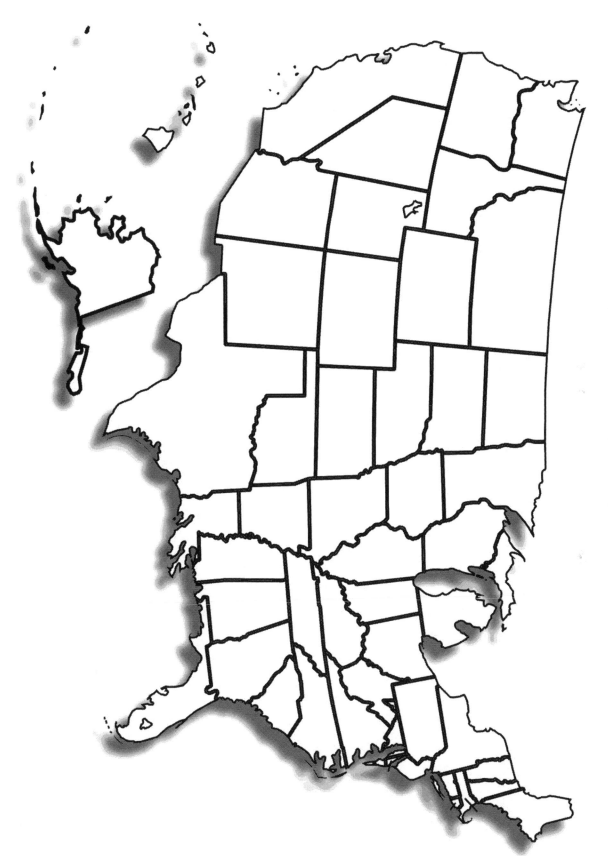

Use a phone, tablet or laptop to identify the 50 US states.

Egypt

Use a phone, tablet or laptop to answer these questions.

1. What is the national motto? _____

2. How many people live there? _____

3. How big is this country? _____

4. Who is the leader? _____

5. Where is the capitol? _____

6. Which city is the largest? _____

7. How long have they been a country? _____

8. What job or work is most common? _____

9. What religion is most popular? _____

10. What are three interesting things you learned? _____

_____

_____

_____

_____

_____

_____

_____

_____

SOURCE: _____

SOURCE: _____

SOURCE: _____

The Flag of Hawaii

Draw the **state flag** of Hawaii. Use colored pencils, crayons, or markers. Be neat and accurate.

Things I learned about Israel

Use a phone, tablet or laptop to learn interesting facts about Israel.

_____
_____
_____
_____
_____
_____
_____
_____
_____
_____
_____
_____
_____
_____
_____
_____
_____
_____
_____

_____
_____
_____
_____
_____

Sources: _____
_____

Who is George Lucas?

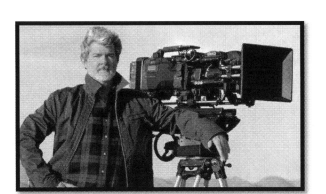

Use a laptop, tablet or phone to access the internet and explore this famous Californian.

Age:

Gender:

Place of birth:

Ethnicity:

Search for interesting facts about this famous Californian: major accomplishments in life, odd jobs, family and marriage, childhood experiences, accidents, anything that you find odd or strange:

ONLINE SOURCES OF INFORMATION:

Historical Facts about North Carolina

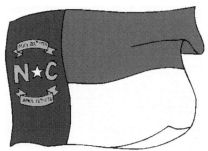

Use a phone, tablet or laptop to discover interesting facts about the history of North Carolina: wars, disasters, laws, accomplishments, challenges...

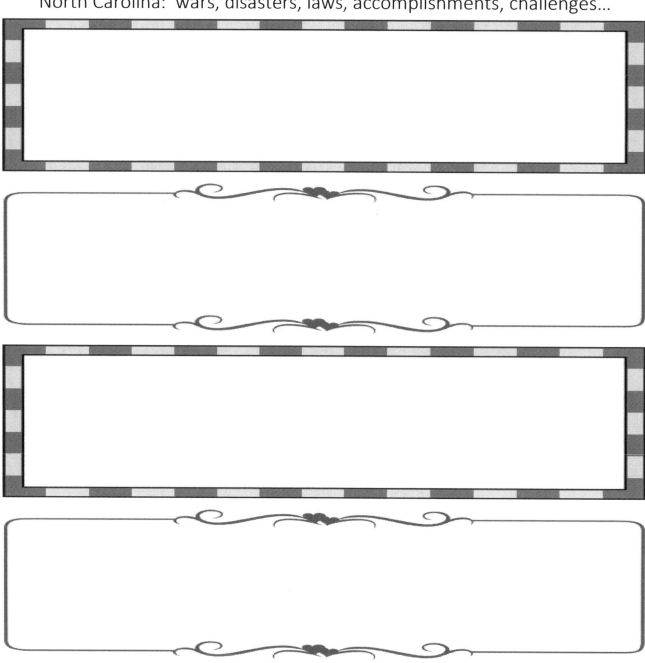

Russian Words

English	Russian
hello	_____
goodbye	_____
bathroom	_____
water	_____
food	_____
help	_____
hospital	_____
police	_____
hotel	_____
me	_____
you	_____
airport	_____
taxi	_____
restaurant	_____
school	_____
office	_____
coffee	_____
computer	_____
telephone	_____
shoe	_____
umbrella	_____
book	_____
library	_____

The Desert Life of Egypt

1

2

3

4

Chinese Words

English	Chinese
hello	_____
goodbye	_____
bathroom	_____
water	_____
food	_____
help	_____
hospital	_____
police	_____
hotel	_____
me	_____
you	_____
airport	_____
taxi	_____
restaurant	_____
school	_____
office	_____
coffee	_____
computer	_____
telephone	_____
shoe	_____
umbrella	_____
book	_____
library	_____

Joshua Tree National Park

What is special about this popular California tourist destination? Why has the US Government set aside this land so that people can visit here and explore? Research online and share what you learn:

1

2

3

4

ONLINE SOURCES OF INFORMATION:

The Appalachian Mountains

Search online for interesting facts about the Appalachian Mountains.

Pony Express National Historic Trail

What is special about this popular California tourist destination? Why has the US Government set aside this land so that people can visit here and explore? Research online and share what you learn:

1. _____
_____
_____
SOURCE: _____

2. _____
_____
_____
SOURCE: _____

3. _____
_____
_____
SOURCE: _____

A Map of Egypt

Use a phone, tablet or laptop to identify important places in this country: mountains, rivers, lakes, cities, historical sites, or bordering countries or bodies of water.

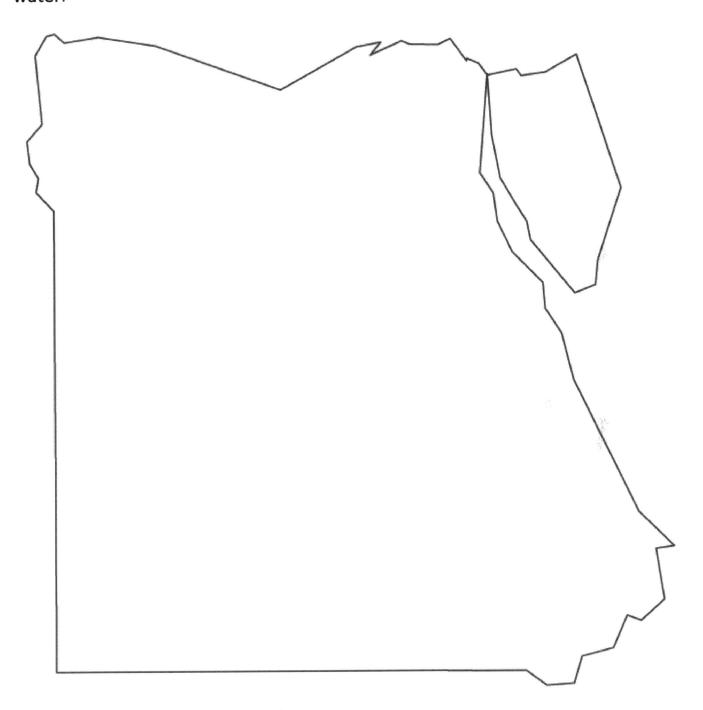

Who is John F. Kennedy?

Use a phone, tablet or laptop to learn five facts about this president and why he is remembered today.

1 _____

2 _____

3 _____

4 _____

5 _____

SOURCES:

_____

The Pigeon

Use a phone, tablet or laptop to answer these questions.

Is the pigeon dangerous to humans?

☐ - YES

☐ - NO

How does a pigeon eat?

Is a pigeon smart?

YES OR **NO**

How long does a pigeon live?

source: _____

source: _____

source: _____

Mother Language Day

International Mother Language Day 21st February

Use a <u>laptop</u>, <u>tablet</u> or <u>phone</u> to access the internet and explore **languages**. Record five interesting facts you learned about the languages people first learn to speak (February 21st).

 ❶

 ❷

 ❸

 ❹

 ❺

Birds

Use a phone, tablet or laptop to answer these questions.

How long does this animal live?

Ostrich: _____

Hummingbird: _____

Owl: _____

Parrot: _____

Where is this animal is born?

Blue Jay: _____

Eagle: _____

Killdeer: _____

Cuckoo: _____

What does this animal eat?

Chickadee: _____

Vulture: _____

Starling: _____

Hawk: _____

What covers the outside of this animal?

Penguin: _____

Hummingbird: _____

Kiwi: _____

Crow: _____

Who is Bill Clinton?

Use a phone, tablet or laptop to answer these questions.

1. When and where was he born? _____
_____
_____

2. What type of work did he do before becoming president? ___
_____
_____

3. Identify several of his accomplishments: _____
_____
_____
_____
_____
_____
_____
_____
_____
_____
_____
_____

SOURCE: _____
SOURCE: _____
SOURCE: _____

Countries in Europe

Use a phone, tablet or laptop to identify some of the largest and most populous countries in Europe:

Austria, Azerbaijan, Belarus, Belgium, Bulgaria, Croatia, Czech Republic, Denmark, England, Finland, France, Russia, Greece, Hungary, Ireland, Kazakhstan, Italy, Netherlands, Norway, Poland, Portugal, Romania, Scotland, Serbia, Slovakia, Spain, Sweden, Switzerland, Turkey, Ukraine, Wales

Wars in Texas

Search online for information about the wars and battles that have occurred in Texas.

_____

_____

_____

_____

_____

_____

_____

_____

_____

_____

_____

_____

_____

ONLINE SOURCES OF INFORMATION:

1)

2)

3)

Mexico

Use a phone, tablet or laptop to answer these questions.

1. What language do they speak? _____
2. How many people live there? _____
3. How big is this country? _____
4. Who is their leader? _____
5. Where is the capitol? _____
6. What kind of money do they use? _____
7. How long have they been a nation? _____
8. What religions are most common? _____
9. What sport is most popular? _____

10. What are three interesting things you learned? _____
_____
_____
_____
_____
_____
_____
_____
_____

SOURCE: _____
SOURCE: _____
SOURCE: _____

The Flag of North Carolina

Draw the **state flag** of North Carolina. Use colored pencils, crayons, or markers. Be neat and accurate.

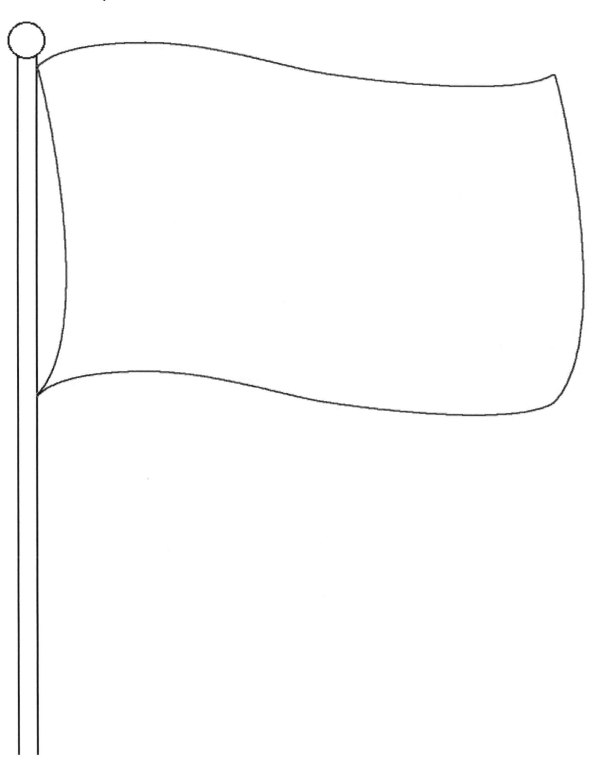

The State Seal of New York

Draw the **Seal** or **Coat of Arms** for this state. Use colored pencils, crayons, or markers. Be neat and accurate.

Things I learned about New York

Use a phone, tablet or laptop to learn interesting facts about New York.

_____

_____

_____

_____

_____

_____

_____

_____

_____

_____

_____

_____

_____

_____

_____

_____

_____

_____

_____

_____

_____

_____

_____

Sources: _____

_____

The Flag of China

Draw the national flag of China. Use colored pencils, crayons, or markers. Be neat and accurate.

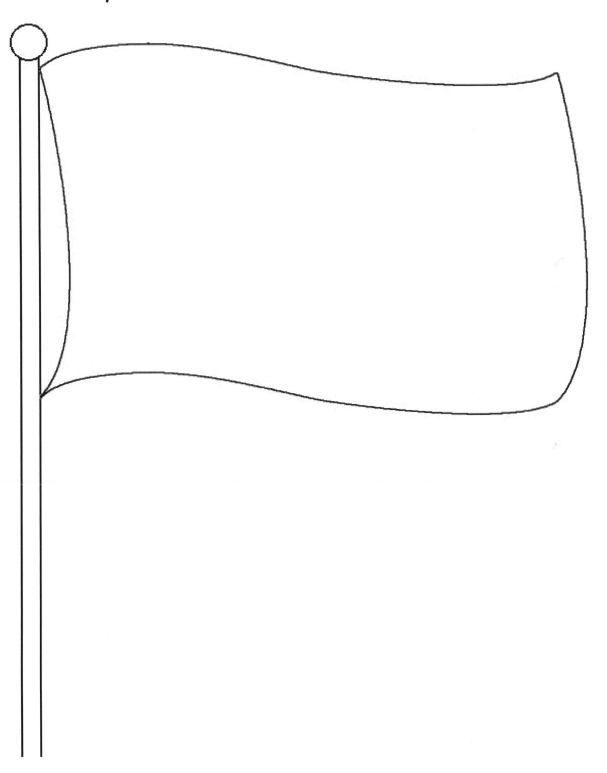

Augustynolophus morrisi

California State Dinosaur

Use a <u>laptop,</u> <u>tablet</u> or <u>phone</u> to access the internet and explore this **dinosaur**. Record several interesting facts you discovered in your research.

SOURCES:

Famous People from Egypt

1

_____

_____

_____

_____

_____

_____

_____

_____

_____

2

_____

_____

_____

_____

_____

_____

_____

_____

_____

3

_____

_____

_____

_____

_____

_____

_____

_____

_____

4

_____

_____

_____

_____

_____

_____

_____

_____

_____

Countries in Africa

Use a phone, tablet or laptop to identify some of the largest and most populous countries in Africa:

Algeria, Angola, Camaroon, Chad, Congo, Egypt, Ethiopia, Ghana, Ivory Coast, Kenya, Liberia, Libya, Madagascar, Mali, Morocco, Mozambique, Niger, Nigeria, Rwanda, Senegal, Sierra Leone, Somalia, South Africa, Sudan, Tanzania, Uganda, Zaire, Zambia, and Zimbabwe

Denim

California State Fabric

Use a <u>laptop</u>, <u>tablet</u> or <u>phone</u> to access the internet and explore this **fabric**. Record several interesting facts you discovered in your research.

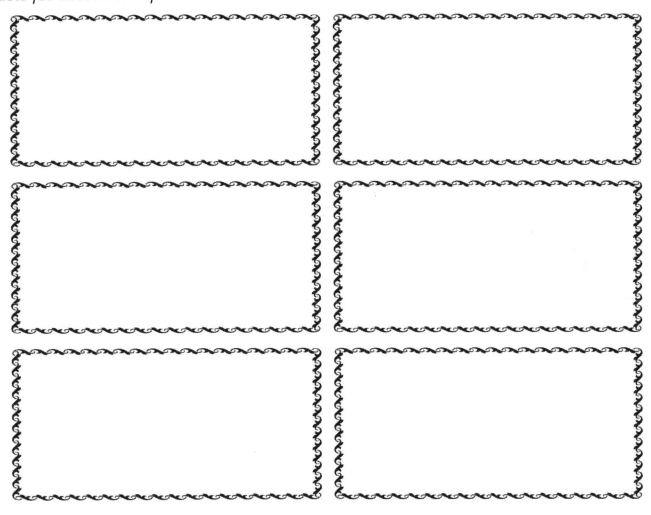

SOURCES:

_____

_____

North Carolina's Culture

Use a phone, tablet or laptop to discover interesting facts about this state.

Food

Music

Clothing

Sports

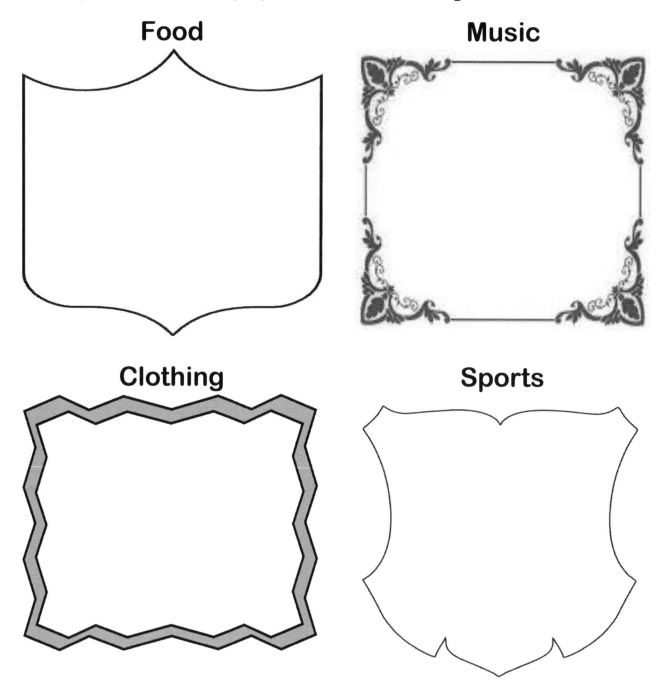

The Coat of Arms of Egypt

Draw the **Coat of Arms** for this country. Use colored pencils, crayons, or markers. Be neat and accurate.

Russia

Use a phone, tablet or laptop to answer these questions.

1. What language do they speak? _____

2. How many people live there? _____

3. How big is this country? _____

4. Who is their leader? _____

5. Where is the capitol? _____

6. What kind of money do they use? _____

7. How long have they been a nation? _____

8. What religions are most common? _____

9. What sport is most popular? _____

10. What are three interesting things you learned? _____

_____

_____

_____

_____

_____

_____

_____

SOURCE: _____

SOURCE: _____

SOURCE: _____

Money from China

Search online for an interesting coin from China. Use colored pencils, crayons or markers as you draw this coin. Be neat and accurate.

Titanic (Belfast)

Search for interesting facts about this Irish tourist destination. What are its most interesting features? Why do people travel there and explore? What is so amazing about this place?

1

2

3

4

ONLINE SOURCES OF INFORMATION: :

Germany

Use a phone, tablet or laptop to learn interesting facts about this country.

Draw the flag for this country.

List five facts you discovered:

1.

2.

3.

4.

5.

List five common wild animals.

Describe a typical resident of this country

Draw a picture that best describes this nation.

Sources: _____

Albert Einstein: Asking Questions

Use a <u>computer</u>, <u>tablet</u> or <u>phone</u> to search online for what people have to say about life's biggest questions. Search for "big questions kids" and see what other people have to say. Read some sites with text and watch a few videos, and then share your thoughts below:

_____

_____

_____

_____

_____

_____

_____

_____

_____

_____

_____

_____

_____

ONLINE SOURCES OF INFORMATION:

_____

_____

California Golden Trout

California State Fish

Use a <u>laptop</u>, <u>tablet</u> or <u>phone</u> to access the internet and explore this **fish**. Record several interesting facts you discovered in your research.

_____

_____

_____

_____

_____

_____

_____

_____

_____

_____

_____

_____

USA

SOURCES:

_____

_____

The State Seal of North Carolina

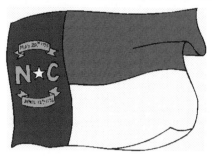

Draw the **Seal** or **Coat of Arms** for this state. Use colored pencils, crayons, or markers. Be neat and accurate.

Reptiles and Amphibians

Use a phone, tablet or laptop to answer these questions.

How long does this animal live?

anaconda: _____

alligator: _____

bullfrog: _____

fence lizard: _____

Where is this animal is born?

rattlesnake: _____

desert tortoise: _____

tree frog: _____

gecko: _____

What does this animal eat?

mamba: _____

box turtle: _____

crocodile: _____

iguana: _____

What covers the outside of this animal?

cobra: _____

komodo dragon: _____

sea turtle: _____

anole: _____

A Stamp from Egypt

Search online for an **interesting stamp** honoring Egypt. Use colored pencils, crayons or markers as you draw this stamp. Be neat and accurate.

Eight Legs

Use a phone, tablet or laptop to answer these questions.

1. What do all spiders produce from their abdomen? _____

_____

_____

source #1: _____

source #2: _____

2. What does a harvestman eat? _____

_____

_____

source #1: _____

source #2: _____

3. Are ticks dangerous to humans? _____

_____

_____

source #1: _____

source #2: _____

4. Why does a scorpion sting hurt? _____

_____

_____

source #1: _____

source #2: _____

5. How small are dust mites? _____

_____

_____

source #1: _____

source #2: _____

National Parks

Search online for ten interesting facts about national parks.

1.

2.

3.

4.

5.

6.

7.

8.

9.

10.

ONLINE SOURCES OF INFORMATION:

_____

_____

How to pan for gold

Explain the process of panning for gold. What does a person do with their <u>hands</u>, <u>feet</u>, and <u>eyes</u>?

_____

_____

_____

_____

_____

_____

_____

_____

_____

_____

ONLINE SOURCES OF INFORMATION:

⬇

_____

_____

Alaska's Flag

Draw the **state flag** of Alaska. Use colored pencils, crayons, or markers. Be neat and accurate.

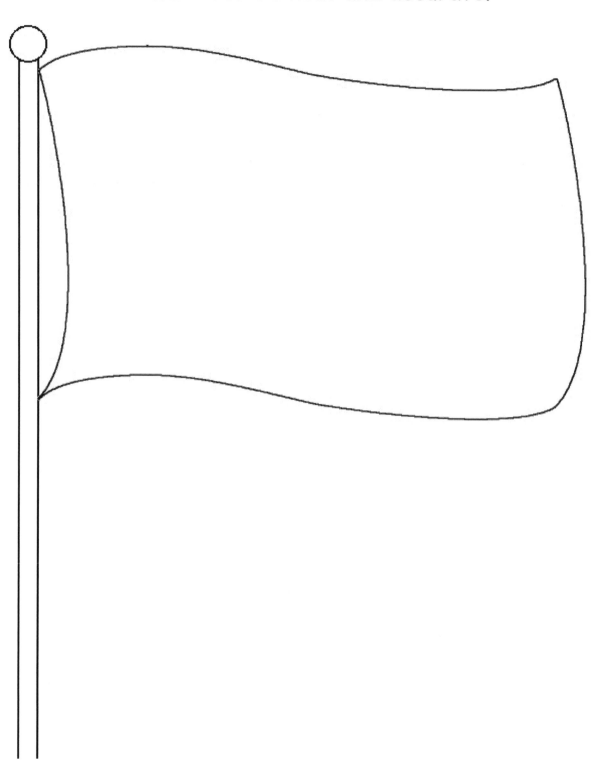

A Coin from Egypt

Search online for a **coin** that honors Egypt. Use colored pencils, crayons or markers as you draw the back of this coin. Be neat and accurate.

Historical Facts about China

Use a phone, tablet or laptop to discover interesting facts about the history of China: wars, disasters, laws, accomplishments, challenges...

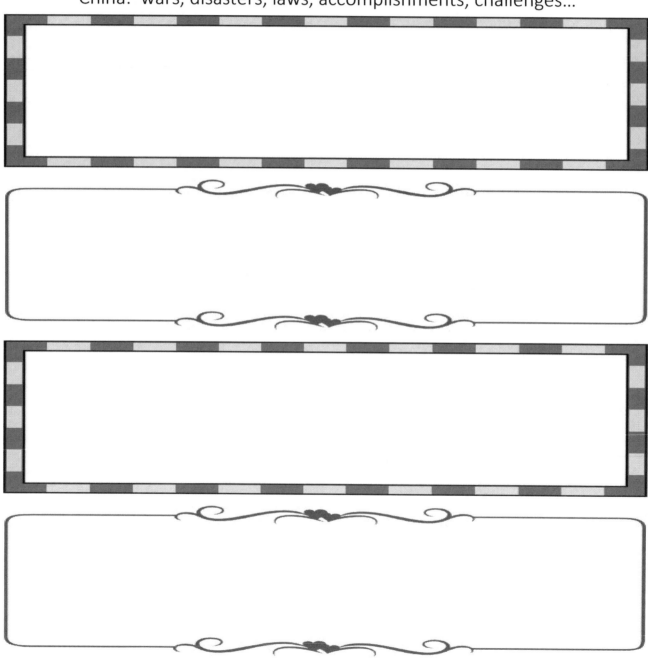

A Stamp from Puerto Rico

Search online for an interesting stamp from Puerto Rico. Use colored pencils,
crayons or markers as you draw this stamp. Be neat and accurate.

The New York Quarter

What WORDS, NUMBERS and PICTURES do you see on this New York quarter and what does each represent? Search online for information about this state.

_____
_____
_____
_____
_____
_____
_____
_____
_____
_____
_____
_____

ONLINE SOURCES OF INFORMATION:

⬇

_____
_____

Trouble

What types of trouble did forty-niners get into out in the woods and beside long rivers?

1. _____
_____
_____
SOURCE: _____

2. _____
_____
_____
SOURCE: _____

3. _____
_____
_____
SOURCE: _____

Supplies

What items did a forty-niner need to bring with him in order to find gold?

 1

 2

 3

 4

ONLINE SOURCES OF INFORMATION:

U.S. Stamp honoring North Carolina

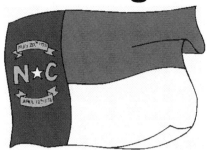

Search online for an **interesting stamp** honoring North Carolina. Use colored pencils, crayons or markers as you draw this stamp. Be neat and accurate.

Protecting the Land

Search online for ten ways that we can protect the land and its natural inhabitants.

1.

2.

3.

4.

5.

6.

7.

8.

9.

10.

ONLINE SOURCES OF INFORMATION:

Yosemite National Park

Obverse

Reverse

What do you notice about the front (obverse) and back (reverse) of this coin?

1

2

3

The Winter Olympics

Use a <u>laptop</u>, <u>tablet</u> or <u>phone</u> to access the internet and explore the **Winter Olympics**. Record five interesting things you learned about this globally-attended event in February.

1

2

3

4

5

Family Day

Use a <u>laptop</u>, <u>tablet</u> or <u>phone</u> to access the internet and explore what it means to be a **Family**. Record several interesting things you discovered below (February 11th).

_____
_____
_____
_____
_____
_____
_____
_____
_____
_____
_____
_____
_____
_____
_____

The Ohlone Tribe

What is special about this indigenous tribe of California? Go online and search for information about their <u>history</u> and <u>people</u>, their <u>religion</u> and where they <u>lived</u>, their <u>leaders</u> and the <u>language</u> they spoke.

 1

 2

 3

 4

ONLINE SOURCES OF INFORMATION:

1)	2)	3)

The Wildlife of Egypt

Draw the national bird, tree, flower and insect of Egypt. Use colored pencils, crayons, or markers. Be neat and accurate.

Bird

Tree

Flower

Insect

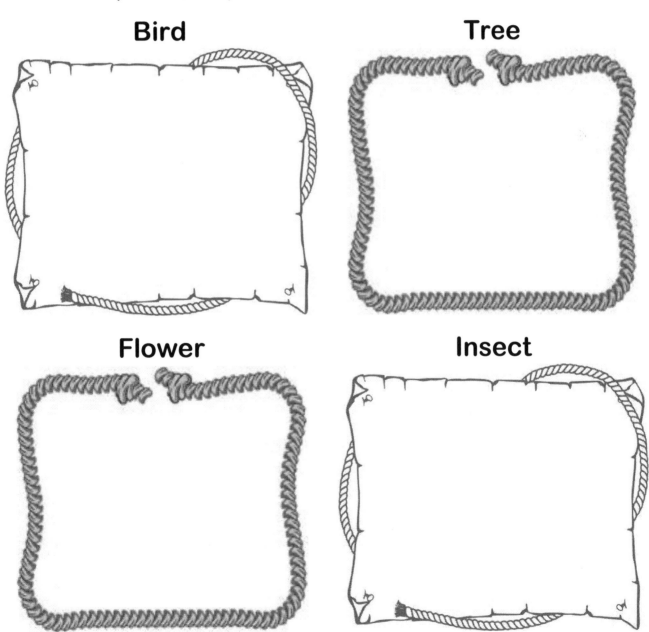

The Paiute Tribe

What is special about this indigenous tribe of California? Go online and search for information about their <u>history</u> and <u>people</u>, their <u>religion</u> and where they <u>lived</u>, their <u>leaders</u> and the <u>language</u> they spoke.

1

2

3

4

ONLINE SOURCES OF INFORMATION: :

_____

_____

Bunratty Castle

Search for interesting facts about this Irish tourist destination. What are its most interesting features? Why do people travel there and explore? What is so amazing about this place?

ONLINE SOURCES OF INFORMATION:

Countries in Latin America

Use a phone, tablet or laptop to identify 22 Latin American countries:

Argentina, Belize, Bolivia, Brazil, Chile, Colombia, Costa Rica, Dominican Republic, Ecuador, El Salvador, French Guiana, Guatemala, Guyana, Honduras, Mexico, Nicaragua, Panama, Paraguay, Peru, Suriname, Uruguay, and Venezuela

The California State Quarter

California State Quarter

Use a <u>laptop</u>, <u>tablet</u> or <u>phone</u> to access the internet and explore this **coin**. Record several interesting facts you discovered in your research about why these images and words are on the quarter.

1

2

3

4

SOURCES:

U.S. Coin honoring North Carolina

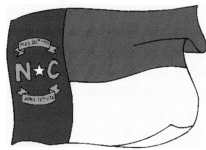

Search online for the **U.S. quarter** that honors North Carolina. Use colored pencils, crayons or markers as you draw the back of this coin. Be neat and accurate.

Eureka!

California State Motto

Use a <u>laptop</u>, <u>tablet</u> or <u>phone</u> to access the internet and explore this **motto**. Record several interesting facts you discovered in your research about this word and who said it in history.

SOURCES:

The Patwin Tribe

What is special about this indigenous tribe of California? Go online and search for information about their <u>history</u> and <u>people</u>, their <u>religion</u> and where they <u>lived</u>, their <u>leaders</u> and the <u>language</u> they spoke.

1. _____
   _____
   _____
   SOURCE: _____

2. _____
   _____
   _____
   SOURCE: _____

3. _____
   _____
   _____
   SOURCE: _____

Who is Nancy Pelosi?

Use a laptop, tablet or phone to access the internet and explore this California politician.

Age:

Gender:

Place of birth:

Ethnicity:

Political affiliation:

Job title:

Search for three interesting facts that you learned about them in your research:

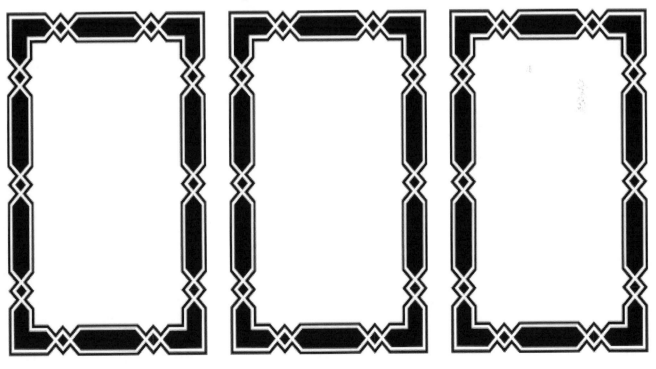

SOURCES:

The Culture of Egypt

Use a phone, tablet or laptop to discover interesting facts about this country.

Food

Music

Clothing

Sports

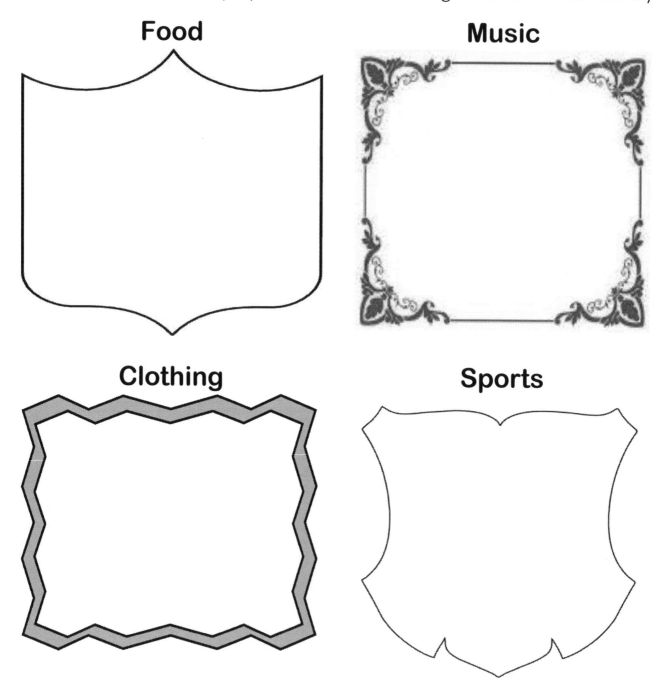

Who is Diane Feinstein?

Use a laptop, tablet or phone to access the internet and explore this California politician.

Age:

Gender:

Place of birth:

Ethnicity:

Political affiliation:

Job title:

Search for four interesting facts that you learned about them in your research:

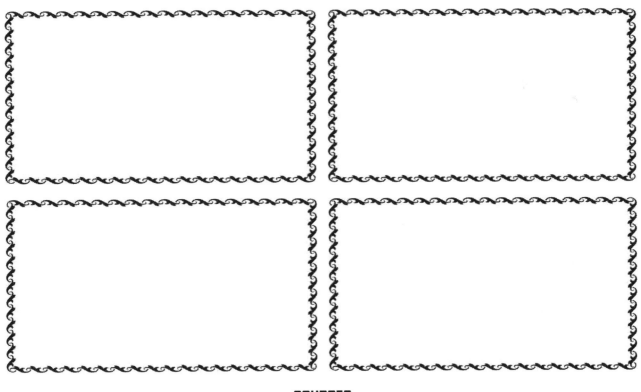

SOURCES:

_____

_____

The Pit River Tribe

What is special about this indigenous tribe of California? Go online and search for information about their <u>history</u> and <u>people</u>, their <u>religion</u> and where they <u>lived</u>, their <u>leaders</u> and the <u>language</u> they spoke.

1

2

3

4

ONLINE SOURCES OF INFORMATION:

1)

2)

3)

The Wildlife of North Carolina

Draw the state bird, tree, flower and insect of North Carolina. Use colored pencils, crayons, or markers. Be neat and accurate.

Bird

Tree

Flower

Insect

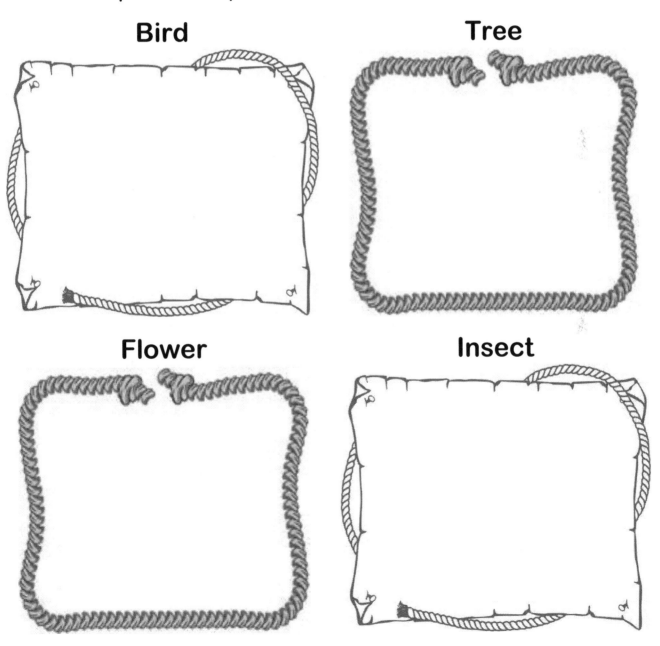

Interesting Facts about Puerto Rico

Use a phone, tablet or laptop to discover interesting facts about the history of this country: wars, disasters, laws, accomplishments, challenges...

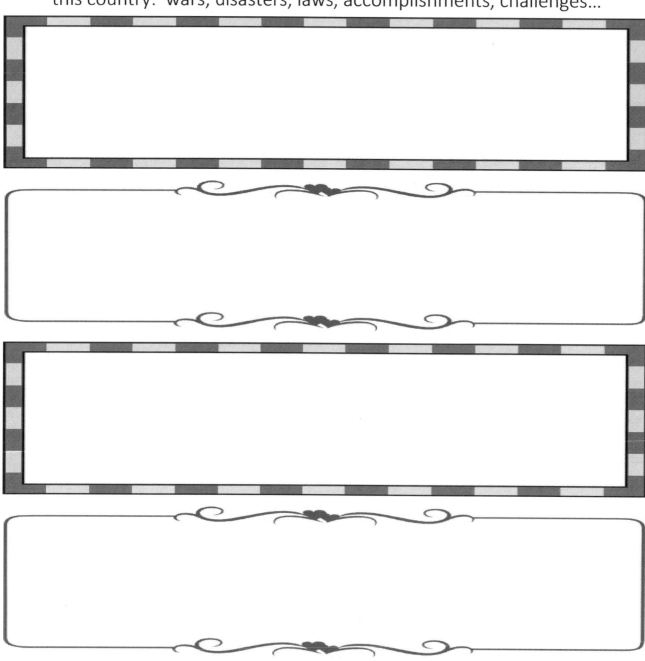

Who is George Washington Carver?

Use a phone, tablet or laptop to learn about this scientist and why he is remembered today.

_____
_____
_____
_____
_____
_____
_____
_____
_____
_____
_____
_____
_____
_____
_____
_____
_____
_____

SOURCES:
_____
_____

Historical Facts about Egypt

Use a phone, tablet or laptop to discover interesting facts about the history of Egypt: wars, disasters, laws, accomplishments, challenges…

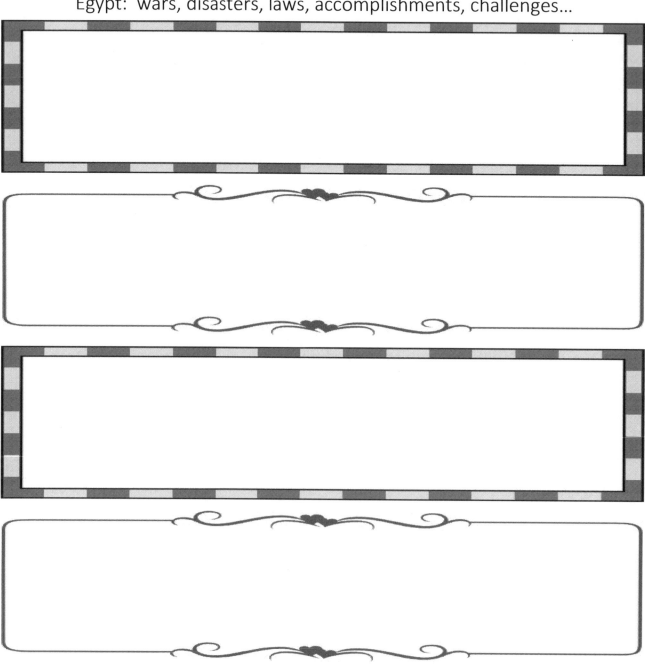

Who is Richard Feynman?

Use a phone, tablet or laptop to learn seven facts about this scientist and why he is remembered today.

1

2

3

4

5

6

7

SOURCES:

_____

_____

The Pomo Tribe

What is special about this indigenous tribe of California? Go online and search for information about their <u>history</u> and <u>people</u>, their <u>religion</u> and where they <u>lived</u>, their <u>leaders</u> and the <u>language</u> they spoke.

 1

2

3

4

ONLINE SOURCES OF INFORMATION:

Famous People from China

Countries in the Middle East

Use a phone, tablet or laptop to identify the countries of the Middle East:

Egypt, Iran, Turkey, Iraq, Saudi Arabia, Yemen, United Arab Emirates, Israel, Jordan, Palestine, Lebanon, Oman, Kuwait, Qatar, and Bahrain.

The Anaconda

Use a phone, tablet or laptop to answer these questions.

Is the anaconda dangerous to humans?

☐ – YES

☐ – NO

How does an anaconda eat?

Is an anaconda smart?

YES
OR
NO

How long does an anaconda live?

24 365 7

source: _____

source: _____

source: _____

Internet Safety

1

Do your work. Don't play around. You have an assignment to do, so focus your attention where it is supposed to be.

2

Search for answers to the questions. Don't get caught going down rabbit holes in search of weird or strange stuff.

3

Imagine that your mother is sitting on your right and your teacher is sitting on your left, watching what you're doing. What would they say to you right now? Make good choices.

This workbook is part of a series:

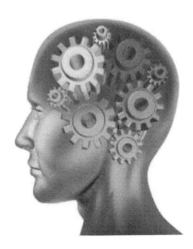

✓ Back to School Internet Research Projects (Grades 5-8)

✓ Christmas Vacation Internet Research Projects (Grades 5-8)

✓ Spring Break Internet Research Projects (Grades 5-8)

✓ End of School Internet Research Projects (Grades 5-8)

✓ Summer Vacation Internet Research Projects (Grades 5-8)

✓ Middle School Internet Research Projects (Grades 5-8)

✓ Junior High Internet Research Projects (Grades 5-8)

Each workbook is filled with 101 different activities to explore animals, people, foreign countries, U.S. states, athletes, singers, politicians, actors, holidays, Native Americans, postage stamps, coins, flags, maps, and so much more. All are available at Amazon.

66554153R00060

"We have the whole pool to ourselves," said Arthur.
"It's a good thing, too," said D.W. "Our bathtub is
bigger than this!"

That night at dinner, everyone ordered lobster.
"Buster loves lobster!" said Arthur.
"*This* is lobster?" said D.W. "I want a hot dog."

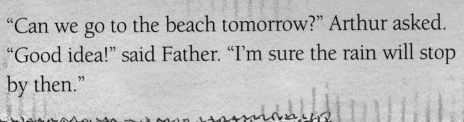

"Can we go to the beach tomorrow?" Arthur asked.
"Good idea!" said Father. "I'm sure the rain will stop
by then."

"No beach today!" D.W. announced the next morning.

"I had a dream about Buster," said Arthur.

"Why don't you write him a postcard?" Mother suggested.

"Why don't we all write postcards?" said Father.

"But what do we write about?" said D.W. "We haven't done anything yet!"

Dear Buster,
I bet you're having fun at camp.
I wish I were there.
Your best friend,
Arthur

POST CARD

PLACE STAMP HERE

Buster
Camp Meadowcroak

Dear Grandma Thora,
You were smart to stay home!
XXXoXoXo
Love,
D.W. xxx ooo xxoxxXo

PLACE STAMP HERE

POST CARD

Grandma Thora
47 Oakmont St.

"What do we do now?" said D.W. "This vacation is a disaster."

At camp there's always something fun to do, thought Arthur. Even on rainy days.

"That's it!" he said. "I'm taking us on a field trip."

"I never heard of a *cow* festival," D.W. said. "But at least it's more fun than our motel room."

"Say 'cheese,'" said Father.

"Let's hurry or we'll miss the milking contest," said Arthur.

For the next few days, it rained and rained, but Arthur didn't mind. He was too busy planning new places to go. He forgot all about missing Buster.

On Wednesday, they went to Gatorville.
"At least the alligators get to swim," said D.W.

Thursday was busy, too. After touring Flo's Fudge Factory, they all went on Jimmy's Jungle Cruise.

"I never realized there are so many fun things to do in the rain," said Father.

"I want to plan a field trip, too," said D.W. "To the movies."

But when they got there, D.W. was too scared to watch.
"I thought it was a movie about fish," she whispered.

Finally, on Friday, their last day, the sun came out.
"What a day!" said Father.
"Just glorious!" said Mother.
Even D.W. was having fun.

No one wanted to leave, but the next day, they packed up and headed home.

"We're almost there," said Mother.

"Phew!" said D.W. "I really have to go to the bathroom."

"Oh, boy," said Arthur, "I can't wait to see Buster."

As soon as they got home, the doorbell rang.

It was Buster.

"Camp was fun, but I missed you," he said to Arthur.

"How was your vacation? How did you and D.W. get along?"

"Great!" said Arthur. "Take a look."

"Wow!" said Buster. "You really did have a great time."